This student workbook is intended to reinforce your understanding of the content in the six modules (B3, C3, P3, B4, C4 and P4) on the new single award GCSE Additional Science B specification (J641), from OCR's Gateway Science Suite.

Every worksheet is cross-referenced to the revision guide, *OCR Gateway GCSE Additional Science Revision Plus,* published by Lonsdale.

You are expected to be able to recall scientific explanations, theories and models in your exams, and demonstrate an understanding of the impact of science on society. To reflect this, the questions and activities in this workbook focus on these key areas. They are varied in style to keep your study interesting and have limited space for answers, so you will have to think carefully about your answers.

HT Throughout this workbook, any questions covering content that is limited to the Higher Tier exam papers appear inside a shaded box, clearly labelled with the symbol **HT**.

At the end of the book, you will find a detailed periodic table which will provide a useful reference as you work through the chemistry worksheets.

A Note to Teachers

The pages in this workbook can be used as...
* classwork sheets – students can use the revision guide to answer the questions
* harder classwork sheets – pupils study the topic and then answer the questions without using the revision guide
* easy-to-mark homework sheets – to test pupils' understanding and reinforce their learning
* the basis for learning homework tasks which are then tested in subsequent lessons
* test materials for topics or entire units
* a structured revision programme prior to the objective tests / written exams.

Answers to these worksheets are available to order.

ISBN 978-1-905129-7. . .

Published by Lonsdale, a division of Huveaux Plc

Authors: Jacquie Punter, Robert Johnson and Steve Langfield

Project Editor: Rachael Hemsley

Cover and Concept Design: Sarah Duxbury

Design: Typehouse

Contents

Contents

Molecules of Life

1 The diagram below shows a typical animal cell. Listed are five parts of the cell and a description of each part. By drawing lines…

a) label the cell

b) link each part of the cell to its description.

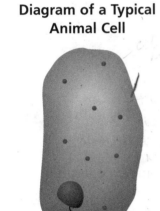

Diagram of a Typical Animal Cell

Part of the Cell	Description
Cell membrane	Most chemical reactions take place here.
Cytoplasm	Controls the cell.
Nucleus	Controls the movement of substances into and out of the cell.
Mitochondrion	Respiration reactions take place here providing energy for the cell.
Ribosomes	Amino acids are joined together to make proteins here.

2 Connect each term to its correct definition.

Nucleus	Different forms of the same gene.
Chromosome	Cell structure that contains the chromosomes.
Gene	Consists of a large number of genes.
Alleles	Small piece of DNA that controls the development of a characteristic.

3 The DNA fingerprint below shows the DNA of a mother and her child, and also two men who both claim to be the child's father. Which man is the child's real father?

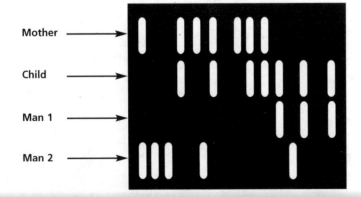

Mother

Child

Man 1

Man 2

....

Molecules of Life

HT

1 a) Label the bases on the opposite strand of DNA.

G	A	A	T	C	T	A	C	A

☐ ☐ ☐ ☐ ☐ ☐ ☐ ☐ ☐

b) The sequence of bases in a gene codes for the sequence of amino acids in a specific protein.

i) How many bases code for one amino acid? ....

ii) How many amino acids would be coded for by the section of DNA shown?

....

2 a) What is the difference between an essential and a non-essential amino acid?

....

....

b) Explain what is meant by a 'first class' source of protein in the diet.

....

....

c) What is the name of the process which the body uses to convert one amino acid into another?

....

3 The cell must copy its DNA molecules exactly before it can divide.

Number the stages **1–4** to put them into the correct order to describe DNA replication.

a) New bases pair up with the exposed bases on the existing DNA strands. ☐

b) The DNA double helix unzips. ☐

c) Two identical pieces of DNA are formed. ☐

d) An enzyme bonds the complementary bases to seal the two new strands together. ☐

4 There are four stages involved in making a DNA fingerprint. Match the name of the process to the correct description.

Separation	The DNA fingerprint is compared to a reference sample of DNA.
Isolation	The DNA is cut into fragments using restriction enzymes.
Comparison	The DNA sections are separated using a technique called electrophoresis.
Fragmentation	DNA is extracted from blood, hair follicles or semen.

Molecules of Life

1 In an experiment, yeast was added to a sugar solution. The number of bubbles of gas given off in one minute was recorded at various temperatures of the sugar solution. The table of results is shown below.

Temperature (°C)	0	10	20	30	40	50	60	70	80
Number of bubbles in one minute	0	10	24	40	48	38	8	0	0

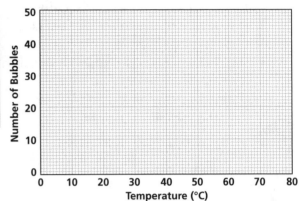

a) Plot a graph of these results on the graph paper.

b) What is the name given to a biological catalyst?

....

c) Describe how the number of bubbles produced varies with the temperature of the sugar solution.

....

d) At what temperature is the number of bubbles produced at its maximum? ....

2 a) 'Different enzymes have different optimum working temperatures.' What does this mean?

....

b) **i)** Explain why enzymes stop working above a certain temperature.

....

ii) Why do enzymes work more slowly as the temperature of their environment decreases?

....

iii) Why do enzymes in saliva probably stop working once they reach the stomach?

....

HT

3 a) Explain what is meant by the 'lock and key' mechanism.

....

b) Name two ways in which a protein molecule can be denatured.

....

1 Explain what is meant by the term 'diffusion'.

....

....

....

2 **a)** Oxygen and carbon dioxide diffuse in or out of plant leaves at different times of the day.

Add two arrows to the diagram alongside to show the direction of diffusion of...

   i) carbon dioxide during the day.

   ii) oxygen during the day.

b) Why does the direction of diffusion of carbon dioxide and oxygen change at night?

....

....

c) Explain the role of diffusion in the loss of water from plant leaves.

....

....

....

HT

3 Tick the box next to the correct option to complete each of the following sentences.　☐

  a) When molecules diffuse...　☐

    i) they all move from an area of high concentration to an area of low concentration.

    ii) they all move from an area of low concentration to an area of high concentration.　☐

    iii) they move randomly in all directions but generally from an area of low concentration to an area of high concentration.

  b) The rate of diffusion is increased when...　☐

    i) there is a smaller surface area of cell membrane.　☐

    ii) there is a greater difference between concentrations (a steeper gradient).　☐

    iii) the particles have a longer distance to travel.

  c) Plant stomata open...　☐

    i) during the day to allow carbon dioxide to diffuse into the leaf.　☐

    ii) at night to allow water to diffuse out of the leaf.　☐

    iii) at night to allow carbon dioxide to diffuse into the leaf.

Diffusion

1 a) Gaseous exchange takes place in the lungs. Which two gases are exchanged?

i) _____ ii) _____

b) Which feature of the lungs allows efficient gaseous exchange to take place?

_____

2 List the substances that diffuse across the placenta…

a) from mother to foetus.

_____

b) from foetus to mother.

_____

HT

3 a) Describe the movement of gases across the wall of the alveoli.

_____

_____

b) With the aid of a diagram, explain how the alveoli are specially adapted for gaseous exchange.

_____

_____

_____

_____

4 How is the inner surface of the small intestine specially adapted for the absorption of dissolved foodstuffs? Explain in as much detail as you can. Draw a diagram in the box to help you make your explanation as clear as possible.

_____

_____

_____

1 The four components of blood are given in the first column of the table below. Complete the table.

Component	Does it have a nucleus?	Function
Plasma		
White blood cell		
Red blood cell		
Platelet		

2 Red and white blood cells are very well adapted for their specific functions. Match the characteristics to the correct cell:

Contains haemoglobin to transport oxygen.

Has biconcave shape to increase surface area for contact with oxygen.

Has flexible shape to engulf pathogens.

Has no nucleus to increase space for haemoglobin.

3 The diagram alongside shows the circulation system.

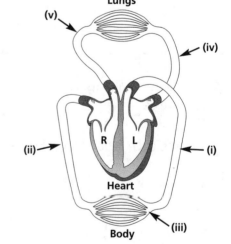

a) What is the function of the circulation system?

b) Name the type of blood vessels labelled.

i)

ii)   iii)

iv)   v)

c) On the diagram, colour deoxygenated blood blue and oxygenated blood red.

d) Clearly label, with arrows, the direction of blood flow around the circulation system.

Keep it Moving

1 Label the diagram of the heart using the labels from the word list.

Lungs

| Body |

| Right atrium |

| Left atrium |

| Right ventricle |

| Left ventricle |

| Semilunar valve |

| Bicuspid valve |

| Tricuspid valve |

Blood to the...

Blood to the...

Blood from the...

Blood from the...

2 a) Why do the ventricles have larger and more muscular walls than the atria?

....

b) Why does the left ventricle have a more muscular wall than the right ventricle?

....

HT

3 The diagrams alongside show two types of blood vessel:

A   B

a) Name each type of blood vessel.

A ....

B ....

b) Why does blood vessel A have a thick elastic, muscular wall?

....

c) Which of the vessels carries blood at high pressure?

....

1 Name three foods that contain a lot of saturated fat and cholesterol.

....

2 Cholesterol build-up in arteries can block the flow of blood. If this happens in the heart it can cause a heart attack.

a) Name the arteries in the heart which can become blocked with cholesterol. ....

b) How does this blockage affect the heart muscle?

....

3 Some problems with a diseased heart can be repaired. Describe the treatment and the aftercare needed for the problems in the table:

Problem	Treatment	Care required after treatment
Irregular or slow heartbeat		
Leaky valves		

4 A transplant patient must take immunosuppressant drugs for the rest of their life. Why does the patient need these drugs?

....

HT

5 Many more patients receive pacemakers or valve replacements than get a heart transplant.
a) Give two reasons why a heart transplant is difficult.

....

....

b) Give two reasons why it is easier to get a pacemaker implanted.

....

Divide and Rule

1 The diagrams alongside show a single-celled organism (an amoeba) and a multi-cellular organism (a horse).

Give two reasons why a multi-cellular organism is so much larger than a single-celled organism.

....

....

....

....

An amoeba

A horse

2 Connect the words 'mitosis' and 'meiosis' to the correct statements.

Cell division.

Involved in asexual reproduction.

Produces cells with the same number of chromosomes.

Mitosis

Involved in sexual reproduction.

Meiosis

Produces gametes with half the number of chromosomes.

Produces genetically identical clones.

Increases variation in offspring.

3 a) How many chromosomes are found in human skin cells? ....

b) How many chromosomes are found in sperm cells? ....

c) What is a cell with two sets of chromosomes called? ....

d) What is a cell with only one set of chromosomes called? ....

4 Insert words in the gaps to complete the following sentences:

Eggs and sperm are .... They are .... cells because they contain only one

set of chromosomes. Eggs and sperm are produced in the ovaries and testes by............................... .

Divide and Rule

5 List two ways that each of these specialised gamete cells is adapted to its function:

a) Egg ....

....

b) Sperm ....

....

6 'Sexual reproduction promotes variation'. Explain how.

....

....

....

....

7 The following statements refer to mitosis. Complete the explanation by drawing a diagram to support each statement.

Parent cell with two pairs of chromosomes	Each chromosome replicates itself	The cell divides for the only time	Genetically identical daughter cells are formed

8 Complete the table to compare the differences between mitosis and meiosis:

Mitosis	Meiosis
Cell divides only once.	
	Pairs of chromosomes move to the poles of the cell for the first division.
Cells are identical clones.	
	Haploid gametes are produced.

Growing Up

1 **a)** The diagram below shows a typical plant cell. Label the plant cell.

b) The diagram represents a palisade cell from a leaf. In what ways are palisade cells specialised to do their job?

....

....

....

c) **i)** Name the structures that are found only in plant cells (not animal cells).

....

ii) Name the structures that are found in both plant and animal cells.

....

2 Put a tick in the boxes next to the statements which are correct.

a) Stem cells can come from animals or plants. ☐

b) Stem cells are undifferentiated or unspecialised cells. ☐

c) Stem cells from adult animals can differentiate into any type of cell. ☐

d) Stem cells from embryos can differentiate into any type of cell. ☐

3 Give three potential uses of human stem cells.

....

....

....

4 Some people object to the use of embryonic stem cells for scientific research. Give one argument for, and one argument against using stem cells in this way:

For: ....

Against: ....

Growing Up

1 The gestation period for an elephant is 700 days; the gestation period for a mouse is only 19 days.

a) What is meant by 'gestation period'? ....

b) Why is there such a difference between the gestation periods of a mouse and an elephant?

....

2 a) Name the five stages of human growth.

....

....

b) At which stage is growth…

i) slowest? .... **ii)** fastest? ....

3 Young children grow very quickly up to the age of two years and then their rate of growth slows down. They have another growth spurt during adolescence.

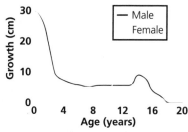

a) Use the graph to find the age at which the average adolescent growth spurt occurs for…

i) girls. ....

ii) boys. ....

b) Why is there a difference between girls and boys?

....

4 a) Why is a baby's head circumference measured regularly? ....

....

....

b) The baby will also be weighed at regular check-ups. What does the weight-to-length measurement show?

....

....

Controlling Plant Growth

1 **a)** State two things that plants are sensitive to.

....

....

The diagram below shows a bean which has just begun to germinate.

b) In what way does…

  i) the root respond to gravity?

  ....

  ii) the shoot respond to gravity?

  ....

  iii) the shoot respond to light?

  ....

c) Which of numbers **i)** to **iii)** from part **b)** (above) are examples of…

  i) geotropism? ....   **ii)** phototropism? ....

d) Describe how hormones control the direction of growth of…

  i) the root ....

  ii) the shoot ....

2 Plant hormones are used in agriculture to control the speed of plant growth.

a) Describe two examples where plant hormones are used to speed up plant growth.

....

....

b) Describe two examples where plant hormones are used to slow down plant growth.

....

....

New Genes for Old

1 What is a mutation? ....

2 The appearance of wheat plants has changed significantly in the last few hundred years.

a) What are the main advantages of the modern-day wheat plant over its predecessor?

....

Wheat Plant   **Modern Day Wheat Plant**

b) State one additional characteristic that would be useful for modern day wheat plants to possess.

....

c) Explain, in as much detail as possible, how the modern wheat plant was developed.

....

....

3 A farmer wants to modify his milk yield to get high volumes of creamy milk that he can sell to ice-cream makers. At the moment, he keeps two different breeds of cow: one breed produces a lot of low-cream milk, the other breed produces small amounts of high-cream milk. Describe the selective breeding process the farmer should go through to get cows which produce large volumes of creamy milk.

....

....

....

....

HT

4 a) State two advantages of selective breeding.

....

....

b) State two disadvantages of selective breeding.

....

....

New Genes for Old

1 Fill in the missing words to complete the following passage about genetic modification.

Genetic modification is a process in which genetic information from one _____ is transferred into

another. The genes are often transferred at an _____ stage of development, so that the

organism will develop with the desired _____. More organisms with the same characteristics

can be produced if the genetically modified organism is then _____.

2 Give three examples of the genetic modification of organisms.

_____

_____

_____

_____

3 Give one advantage and one disadvantage to genetically modifying of an organism, e.g. genetically modifying a soya plant to make it resistant to pests.

Advantage: _____

Disadvantage: _____

HT

4 State two ethical concerns associated with genetic engineering.

a) _____

b) _____

5 Genetic engineering opens up a number of possibilities for the human race, as well as many possible dangers. Do you think scientists should continue their genetic research? Explain your answer.

_____

_____

_____

_____

More of the Same

1 **a)** In terms of variation, what is the key characteristic of an organism obtained through asexual reproduction?

....

b) Why could this be desirable for commercial plant growers?

....

....

c) Name two plants that can reproduce asexually.

....

2 Discuss the advantages and disadvantages of commercially cloning plants.

....

....

....

3 The diagram below shows the sequence of events used to clone sheep by embryo transplantation. Write a brief description of what is happening at each stage of the process.

| Stage 1 | Stage 2 | Stage 3 | Stage 4 |

Stage 1: ....

....

Stage 2: ....

....

Stage 3: ....

....

Stage 4: ....

....

More of the Same

4 One reason for cloning animals would be to supply organs for transplants for humans. The animals would have to be genetically modified first.

a) Explain why you cannot transplant a normal pig's kidney into a human patient.

....

b) Explain why the animal organ donors would need to be genetically modified.

....

HT

5 a) What is a clone?

....

b) Explain how clones may be produced using tissue culture.

....

....

....

c) Why is it easier to clone plants than animals?

....

....

6 Dolly the sheep (the first successful mammal clone) was cloned from an adult sheep cell, not by embryo cloning and transplantation.

Outline the steps needed in order to clone Dolly the sheep.

....

....

....

....

....

Fundamental Chemical Concepts

1 Unscramble the words below that relate to particles in an atom. Then write down where in an atom you would find each one.

a) TRONPO ....

b) ERENCLOT ....

c) RUTNEON ....

2 Draw lines between the boxes to link the words with their definition.

Reactant	Made of only one type of atom.
Element	Made in a chemical reaction.
Compound	Two elements chemically combined.
Product	A starting material in a chemical reaction.

3 Use a periodic table to look up the names of the following elements.

H: .... O: .... C: .... N: ....

Fe: .... Na: .... Cl: .... K: ....

Al: .... P: .... I: .... Br: ....

4 Complete the table below.

Chemical Symbol	Chemical Name	Elements	Number of Atoms of Each Element
H_2O			
CO_2			
NH_3			

Fundamental Chemical Concepts

1 Look at the displayed formulae, then complete the table.

i)
```
    H
    |
H − C − H
    |
    H
```

ii)
```
    H   H
    |   |
H − C − C − H
    |   |
    H   H
```

iii)
```
    H      O
    |     //
H − C − C
    |      \
    H      O − H
```

iv)
```
 H         H
  \       /
   C = C
  /       \
 H         H
```

	i)	ii)	iii)	iv)
Number of Carbon Atoms				
Number of Hydrogen Atoms				
Number of Oxygen Atoms				
Number of Single Covalent Bonds				
Number of Double Covalent Bonds				

2 Complete the table by writing the formula for each compound:

	Oxide	Carbonate	Chloride	Hydroxide
Copper (II)			$CuCl_2$	
Zinc			$ZnCl_2$	$Zn(OH)_2$
Iron (II)			$FeCl_2$	
Magnesium		$MgCO_3$		

3 Write down the total number of atoms in each of the following formulae:

a) NaOH

b) MgO_2

c) Al_2O_3

d) $Cu(OH)_2$

e) CH_3COOH

Fundamental Chemical Concepts

1 Fill in the missing words that describe the participants in a reaction.

$$A + B \longrightarrow C + D$$

_____ $\longrightarrow$ _____

2 For each of the following chemical reactions...

i) draw the correct number of atoms / molecules under the equation.

ii) write the names of all the substances underneath.

e.g.

$2Na_{(s)}$	+	$2H_2O_{(l)}$	$\longrightarrow$	$2NaOH_{(aq)}$	+	$H_{2(g)}$
	+		$\longrightarrow$		+	
Sodium	+	Water	$\longrightarrow$	Sodium hydroxide	+	Hydrogen

a)

$C_{(s)}$	+	$O_{2(g)}$	$\longrightarrow$	$CO_{2(g)}$
i)	+		$\longrightarrow$	
ii)	+		$\longrightarrow$	

b)

$CH_{4(g)}$	+	$2O_{2(g)}$	$\longrightarrow$	$CO_{2(g)}$	+	$H_2O_{(l)}$
i)	+		$\longrightarrow$		+	
ii)	l		$\longrightarrow$		+	

c)

$CaCO_{3(s)}$	+	$2HCl_{(l)}$	$\longrightarrow$	$CO_{2(g)}$	+	$H_2O_{(l)}$	+	$CaCl_{2(s)}$
i)	+		$\longrightarrow$		+		+	
ii)	+		$\longrightarrow$		+		+	

What Are Atoms Like?

1 Use the following words to complete the paragraph below:

compound **atoms** **nucleus** **protons** **neutrons** **electrons** **element**

All substances are made up of _____ . A substance made from only one type of atom is called

an_____ . When two or more different atoms combine chemically, a _____

is made. All the mass of an atom is concentrated in the_____ which is surrounded by

orbiting _____ . There are two particles in the nucleus of an atom: _____

and_____ .

2 Next to each statement, write down whether it is **true** or **false**.

a) There are over 500 elements. _____

b) The atomic number is the number of protons in an atom. _____

c) An isotope has the same number of neutrons but a different number of protons. _____

d) Mass number = number of protons + number of neutrons. _____

3 Complete the table:

Atomic Particle	Relative Mass	Relative Charge
Proton		+1
	1	
		-1

4 Complete the equations:

a) Atomic Number = Number of _____ = Number of electrons (in a neutral atom)

b) Mass number = Number of _____ + Number of_____

5 What is an isotope?

_____

HT

1 What name is given to…

a) the number of protons in an atom? ....

b) the total number of particles in a nucleus? ....

c) the arrangement of electrons in shells? ....

d) atoms of the same element with different numbers of neutrons? ....

2 Complete the table:

Isotope	Chemical Name	Number of Protons	Number of Electrons	Number of Neutrons
$^{1}_{1}H$		1	1	0
$^{2}_{1}H$				
$^{3}_{1}H$				
$^{37}_{17}Cl$				
$^{35}_{17}Cl$				
$^{235}_{92}U$				

3 Enter in the boxes the maximum number of electrons that each electron shell can contain.

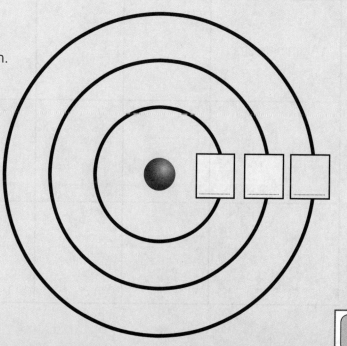

What Are Atoms Like?

1 Below are the electron configurations for eight elements. For each one write down the number of the Period and the Group it belongs to.

a) 2,7   **i)** Period: _____   **ii)** Group: _____

b) 2,8,8   **i)** Period: _____   **ii)** Group: _____

c) 2,4   **i)** Period: _____   **ii)** Group: _____

d) 2,8,2   **i)** Period: _____   **ii)** Group: _____

e) 2,8,6   **i)** Period: _____   **ii)** Group: _____

f) 2,8,8,1   **i)** Period: _____   **ii)** Group: _____

g) 2,2   **i)** Period: _____   **ii)** Group: _____

h) 2,8,5   **i)** Period: _____   **ii)** Group: _____

2 Complete the following table. The first one has been done for you.

Chemical Name and Symbol	Proton Number	Number of Electrons	Electron Configuration	Electron Configuration Diagram
Lithium, Li	3	3	2, 1	•
Aluminium, _____			2, 8, 3	•
Chlorine, _____				•
			2, 3	•

How Atoms Combine – Ionic Bonding

1 a) What is an ion? ....

b) How is a positive ion formed? ....

c) How is a negative ion formed? ....

2 The diagram below shows the structure of sodium chloride. Explain how sodium and chloride atoms combine to form this structure.

....

....

....

....

....

3 Connect the compounds, sodium chloride and magnesium oxide, to the correct statements. (Some of the statements may apply to both.)

| Dissolves in water. |
| Conducts electricity when molten. |

Sodium chloride · | Has a very high melting point. | · Magnesium oxide

| Does not conduct electricity when solid. |
| Conducts electricity when it is in solution. |

HT

4 Explain why…

a) sodium chloride has a high melting point.

....

b) magnesium oxide conducts electricity when molten.

....

c) sodium chloride does not conduct electricity when solid.

....

How Atoms Combine – Ionic Bonding

1 Complete the following table, using the periodic table at the back of the book. (The first one has been done for you.)

Element	Atomic Number	Number of Electrons	Electronic Configuration
Sodium	11	11	2,8,1
Chlorine			
Oxygen			
Magnesium			

2 a) Draw an electron configuration diagram of a sodium atom and a chlorine atom in the boxes below.

b) How does a sodium atom become a sodium ion?

_____

_____

c) How does a chlorine atom become a chloride ion?

_____

_____

d) Draw an electron configuration diagram of sodium chloride, NaCl, in the box alongside.

3 Magnesium reacts with oxygen to form magnesium oxide, MgO.

a) How does an oxygen atom become an oxide ion?

_____

_____

b) Draw electron configuration diagrams for an oxygen atom and an oxide ion in the boxes alongside.

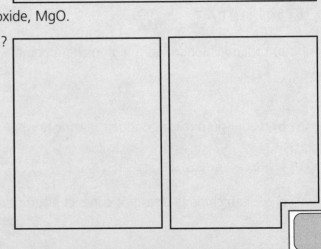

How Atoms Combine – Ionic Bonding

1 Magnesium and chlorine react together to produce magnesium chloride.

$$Mg + Cl_2 \longrightarrow MgCl_2$$

a) Use the periodic table at the back of this book to find the atomic numbers of magnesium and chlorine.

Magnesium: .... Chlorine: ....

b) Magnesium chloride is an ionic compound. Explain how a magnesium atom becomes a magnesium ion.

....

c) Explain how magnesium and chlorine combine to form magnesium chloride.
Draw electron configuration diagrams to help you.

2 For each of the following compounds, three choices of formulae are given. Circle the correct one.

a) Calcium hydroxide: **i)** $CaOH$ **ii)** Ca_2OH **iii)** $Ca(OH)_2$

b) Magnesium oxide: **i)** MgO **ii)** Mg_2O **iii)** MgO_2

c) Aluminium oxide: **i)** AlO **ii)** Al_3O_2 **iii)** Al_2O_3

d) Copper (II) chloride: **i)** $CuCl$ **ii)** Cu_2Cl **iii)** $CuCl_2$

e) Iron (II) sulfate: **i)** $FeSO_4$ **ii)** Fe_2SO_4 **iii)** $Fe(SO_4)_2$

f) Iron (III) sulfate: **i)** Fe_2SO_4 **ii)** $Fe_2(SO_4)_3$ **iii)** $Fe(SO_4)_2$

3 Use your knowledge of the bonding that is used in magnesium chloride to predict some of its properties.

....

....

Covalent Bonding and The Periodic Table

1 a) What is the name given to a horizontal row of elements in the periodic table?

_____

b) What is the name given to a vertical column of elements?

_____

2 a) How many electrons are in the outer shell of an element in Group 1?

_____

b) How many electrons are in the outer shell of an element in Group 7?

_____

3 What is a molecule?

_____

_____

4 Draw lines between the boxes to link the words with their definitions.

| Ionic bonding | | Non-metal with non-metal | | Share electrons |

| Covalent bonding | | Metal with non-metal | | Transfer electrons |

5 Decide whether each of the following statements are **true** or **false** and write the answer on the line alongside.

a) There are about 300 elements. _____

b) The formula of water is H_2O. _____

c) Nearly 80% of all elements are metals. _____

d) The bonding in CO_2 is ionic. _____

e) A row in the periodic table is called a Period. _____

f) A column in the periodic table is called a Group. _____

g) The elements in the periodic table are arranged in increasing order of mass. _____

Covalent Bonding and The Periodic Table

1 a) The diagram opposite shows the electron configurations for hydrogen and oxygen. A molecule of water is made up of 1 atom of oxygen and 2 atoms of hydrogen. Explain how hydrogen and oxygen form a water molecule.

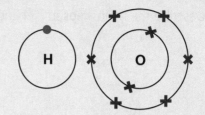

Draw a diagram to support your answer.

....

....

....

....

b) i) What is a single covalent bond? ....

ii) What is a double covalent bond? ....

2 Complete the following table.

Molecule	Formula	Displayed Formula	Dot and Cross Model
Hydrogen		H – H	
Chlorine			
		H $-$ C $-$ H (with H above and H below C)	

3 a) Explain why simple covalently bonded molecules have low melting and boiling points.

....

b) Simple covalently bonded molecules also have another characteristic in common. State what it is and give a reason for it.

....

The Group 1 Elements

1 **a)** Describe the main steps in carrying out a flame test.

_____

_____

_____

_____

_____

b) What colour would the following compounds produce in a flame test?

i) Potassium chloride _____

ii) Lithium sulfate _____

iii) Sodium bromide _____

2 Lithium is the first element in Group 1 of the periodic table. A piece of lithium is placed in a beaker of water. The water has universal indicator solution in it.

a) Why does the lithium float?

_____

_____

b) The colour of the water turns from green to purple. Explain why.

_____

_____

c) Write a word equation for the reaction that takes place between lithium and water.

_____

HT **d)** Write a symbol equation (with state symbols) for the reaction that takes place between lithium and water.

_____

HT

1 The graph below shows the density of the first five elements of Group 1. They are not in order.

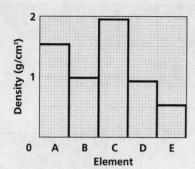

a) Name the five elements shown in the graph.

A: ....

B: ....

C: ....

D: ....

E: ....

b) What trend is there in the density of the alkali metals as we go down the Group?

....

c) Outline one other trend in the physical properties as you go down Group 1.

....

2 **a)** Why would you not carry out the reaction between rubidium and water?

....

b) Predict what you would see if some caesium was added to cold water.

....

3 Draw dots or crosses on the rings in the boxes to show the electron configurations of the atoms and ions of the two alkali metals: sodium and potassium. A sodium atom has 11 electrons and a potassium ion has 18 electrons.

Sodium atom	Sodium ion	Potassium atom	Potassium ion
a) i)	ii)	**b)** i)	ii)

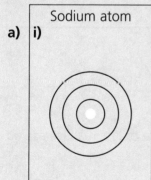 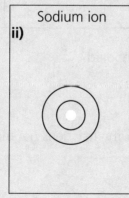 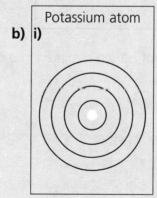 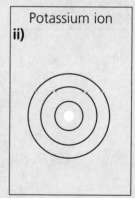

c) Write the symbol equation for the formation of a sodium ion from a sodium atom.

....

The Group 7 Elements

1 Complete the table:

Halogen	Symbol	Colour	State at 250°C	Use
Fluorine		Pale green	Gas	PTFE plastic
Chlorine				
Bromine				Photography
Iodine				

2 Rob carried out an experiment to see how halogens (Group 7) react with halogen compounds. He added aqueous solutions of bromine, iodine and chlorine in turn to aqueous solutions of sodium chloride, sodium bromide and sodium iodide.

a) Complete the table of results. Use a tick (✓) to indicate a reaction, and a cross (✗) to indicate no reaction.

	Sodium Iodide (NaI)	Sodium Chloride (NaCl)	Sodium Bromide (NaBr)
Bromine			
Iodine			
Chlorine			

b) Why was the experiment carried out in a fume cupboard?

c) Using the results of this experiment, state whether the halogens get more or less reactive as you go down the group.

d) Write a balanced symbol equation (with state symbols) for one of the reactions in part a) above.

HT

1 The following table shows the boiling points of the first five elements of Group 7. (They are not in order.)

Element	Boiling Point
A	59°C
B	337°C
C	-188°C
D	184°C
E	-34°C

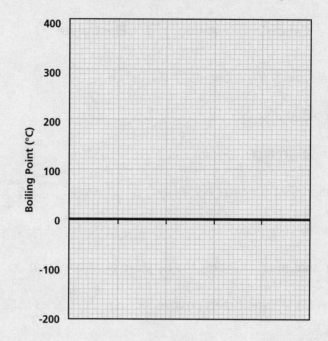

a) Name the five elements.

A:_____   B: _____   C: _____

D: _____   E: _____

b) Draw a bar graph (on the paper provided above) to show the data in the table.

c) What trend is there in the boiling points of the halogens as we go down the group?

_____

2 OILRIG is the best way to remember what happens in reduction and oxidation reactions. What do the letters stand for?

O = _____

I = _____

L = _____ of electrons.

R = _____

I = _____

G = _____ of electrons.

Electrolysis

1 Use the words from the word list below to show what the following statements describe.

| Ion | Cation | Anion | Electrolyte | Electrolysis | Cathode | Anode |

a) Using electricity to decompose a substance. ....

b) A charged atom. ....

c) A negatively charged ion. ....

d) A solution that conducts electricity. ....

e) The positive electrode. ....

f) The ion that moves towards the negative electrode. ....

g) The electrode that attracts positive ions. ....

2 a) In the diagram box, draw the apparatus you would use for the electrolysis of sulfuric acid.

b) Which ion is attracted to the cathode?

....

c) What is made at the cathode?

....

d) Which ion is attracted to the anode?

....

e) What is made at the anode?

....

HT **f)** Write the balanced half-equation for the reaction at the cathode. Is it oxidation or reduction?

....

g) Write the balanced half-equation for the reaction at the anode. Is it oxidation or reduction?

....

1 Describe a simple test you would use to identify the following gases (do not forget to include what the results of the tests mean!):

a) Oxygen ....

....

b) Hydrogen ....

....

2 Aluminium is extracted from its purified ore, aluminium oxide, by electrolysis.

a) Label the diagram, using the following words: **anode, cathode, oxygen ions, aluminium ions**

b) Explain why this method has to be used.

....

....

....

....

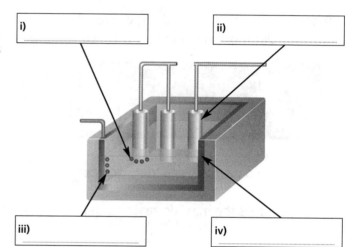

i) ....

ii) ....

iii) ....

iv) ....

c) Why must the aluminium oxide be molten in order for electrolysis to take place?

....

d) What takes place at the anode? ....

e) What takes place at the cathode? ....

f) Why do the anodes have to be replaced fairly frequently? ....

---

^{HT}

3 a) Why is the aluminium oxide mixed with cryolite?

....

b) Is the half-equation below an example of reduction or oxidation?

$$2O^{2-}_{(l)} - 4e^- \longrightarrow O_{2(g)}$$ ....

c) Explain your answer to part b). ....

Transition Elements

1 a) Give the names of five transition metals.

_____

b) List four properties that these metals have in common.

_____

2 What is thermal decomposition?

_____

3 An experiment was carried out where different masses of copper carbonate were heated until they turned from a bluish-green colour to a black colour. The results are shown in the table below.

Mass Before Heating	0.75g	1.25g	0.5g	1.0g	0.25g
Mass After Heating	0.5g	0.8g	0.3g	0.65g	0.16g

a) On the paper provided, draw a graph to show the results.

b) Why does the mass decrease during the experiment?

_____

c) Write a word equation for the reaction that took place.

_____

d) What other simple test could be carried out to show that a thermal decomposition reaction has taken place?

_____

4 a) Describe simply how you would identify whether a compound in solution contains copper (II) ions.

_____

_____

b) Write an ionic symbol equation for the precipitate formed.

_____

Metal Structure and Properties

1 Draw lines between the boxes to link the physical property to the correct metal product.

Conducts heat	Steel cable on a suspension bridge.
High density	Silver earrings.
Hard	Aluminium saucepans.
Strong	Steel drill bits.
Lustrous	Lead diving weights.
Conducts electricity	Brass prongs on a household plug.

2 Use the diagram to help you explain…

a) why metals have a high melting point.

....

....

....

b) how metals can conduct electricity.

....

....

....

3 a) What is a superconductor?

....

b) Outline one use of a superconductor.

....

4 Describe how metal atoms bond together.

....

....

5 Give at least two reasons why superconductors are not used in everyday applications.

....

Speed

1 Calculate the average speed of each of the following:

a) A car that travels 120km in 3 hours.

b) An aeroplane that flies 3600km in 5 hours.

c) A runner that takes 3 min 20s to complete a 1500m race.

d) A world-class sprinter who runs 100m in 9.8s.

2 A walker covers 6km in 1 hour. What is her average speed in metres per second? (Make sure you use the correct units!) Show your working.

HT

3 A car travels at an average speed of 100km/h.
How far would it travel in $2\frac{1}{2}$ hours? Show your working.

4 A coach drives from London to Leeds, which is a distance of 200 miles. The coach averages a speed of 60mph for the first 50 miles, 50mph for the next 90 miles and 40mph for the remainder of the journey. How long does it take the coach to travel from London to Leeds?

5 A jet aircraft travels at an average speed of 550mph. It takes 570 minutes to get to its destination. How far away is the destination? Show your working.

1 Jim and Dom were having an 800m race. Their times were recorded every 100m. The table below shows the results.

Distance Run (m)	100	200	300	400	500	600	700	800
Jim's Time (s)	15	30	45	65	85	105	130	155
Dom's Time (s)	20	40	60	80	95	110	125	140

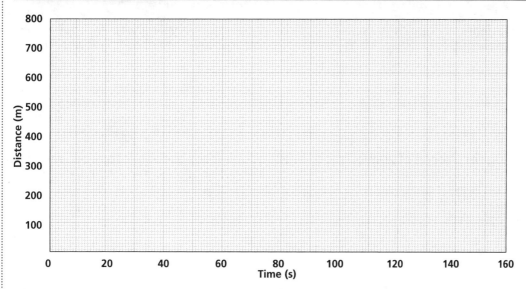

a) Draw the distance–time graphs for both boys' results on the axes above.

b) Between which two times was Jim's speed the slowest? _____

c) Between which two times was Dom's speed the slowest? _____

d) Who won the race and by how many seconds? _____

2 In the space below, sketch a distance–time graph showing a car accelerating at a constant rate from rest.

Changing Speed

1 **a)** What do we mean by the term 'acceleration'? ....

b) What units is acceleration measured in? ....

c) What do we mean by the term 'deceleration'? ....

2 Calculate the acceleration for each of the following. (Show your working, and make sure you use the correct units!)

a) A car that accelerates uniformly from rest to a speed of 15m/s in a time of 5s.

....

....

b) A train that accelerates uniformly from rest and reaches a speed of 30m/s after 15s.

....

....

c) A car that accelerates from a speed of 20m/s to 34m/s in 4s.

....

....

d) A train that accelerates from rest and reaches a speed of 40m/s after 2 minutes.

....

....

3 A fighter plane lands on an aircraft carrier at a speed of 40m/s. It is stopped in a time of 2s. Calculate the deceleration of the fighter plane.

....

HT

4 A car is travelling at 12m/s. It accelerates at a rate of $2m/s^2$ for 10 seconds. Calculate its new speed. Show your working.

....

....

....

5 An object at rest falls from the top of a cliff. It falls through the air with an acceleration of $10m/s^2$ and hits the ground at a speed of 24m/s. How long did it take the object to reach the ground?

....

....

....

Changing Speed

1 The table below shows a motorcyclist's speed at regular intervals as he travels between two sets of traffic lights.

Time (s)	0	2	4	6	8	10	12	14	16	18	20	22
Speed (m/s)	0	5	10	10	10	13	16	16	12	8	4	0

a) Draw a speed–time graph of the motorcyclist's journey on the axes opposite.

b) Between which two times was the motorcyclist's acceleration the greatest?

_____

c) Between which times was the motorcyclist's speed constant?

Between _____ and _____ .

Between _____ and _____ .

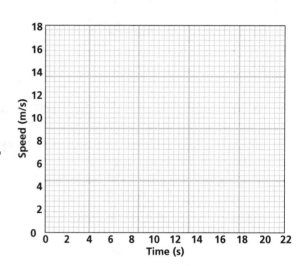

2 The speed–time graph below is for a train moving from one station to the next.

a) Describe the motion of the train.

_____

_____

_____

b) Calculate the two accelerations of the train.

_____

_____

c) Calculate the two decelerations of the train.

_____

_____

d) Calculate the total distance travelled by the train.

_____

Forces and Motion

1 Diagrams A to F show the forces acting on three cars and three lorries.

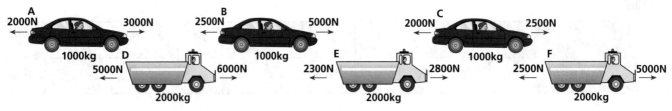

For each of these questions, explain your answer.

a) Which car has the smallest acceleration? ....

b) Which lorry has the greatest acceleration? ....

c) Will car B or lorry F have the greater acceleration? ....

d) Which two vehicles have the same acceleration? ....

2 A motorcyclist is moving along a straight road. The total mass of the motorcyclist and motorcycle is 250kg.

a) The motorcyclist is moving at a constant speed of 20m/s. The value of the driving force is 2000N. What is the value of the resistive force? Explain your answer.

....

....

b) The motorcyclist increases her speed from 20m/s to 30m/s in 5s. Calculate the acceleration of the motorcyclist.

....

c) Calculate the force needed to produce the acceleration in part b) above. ....

....

d) What is the total force produced by the motorcycle during this acceleration? ....

3 A car decelerates from 15m/s to a standstill in 5s. The mass of the car and the driver is 1000kg. Explain how the force required to produce the same deceleration would change if the mass of the car and driver was increased to 1500kg.

....

1 The stopping distance of a vehicle depends on two factors: the distance travelled during the driver's thinking time and the distance travelled during the time the brakes are applied.

a) If a driver's reaction time is 0.75s and the car is travelling at 12m/s, calculate how far the car travels before the driver presses his foot on the brake.

....

....

b) Once the brakes have been pressed it takes another 6 seconds for the car to stop. Calculate the deceleration of the car.

....

....

2 a) List three factors that can increase thinking distance.

....

b) What effect does an increase in thinking distance have on…

i) braking distance? ....

ii) overall stopping distance? ....

3 List three factors that can increase braking distance.

....

HT

4 Draw lines between the boxes to match the changed factor to the effect on braking distance.

| A larger force is applied to the brake pedal. |

| Less force is applied to the brake pedal. |

| It starts raining. |

| The vehicle has more passengers in it. |

| The vehicle is travelling slower. |

| Braking distance is increased. |

| Braking distance is reduced. |

Work and Power

1 Only one of the activities below does not involve doing work. Circle it.

Weight training   **Riding a bike**   **Standing on top of a tall tower**   **Eating lunch**

2 Why should we be concerned if more people buy more powerful cars?

_____

_____

3 A cyclist moves along a flat road against a resistive force of 100N. If the cyclist travels 1000m, calculate how much work he has done.

_____

_____

4 Matt cycles a distance of 2000m against a resistive force of 150N. He travels this distance in 400s.

   a) Calculate how much work is done by Matt.

   _____

   b) What is Matt's power output?

   _____

5 A pumped storage system is used to store water in a dam. Water flows down through the pipes, turning turbines which generate electricity. When there is not much demand for electricity, the water is pumped back up to the top reservoir.

   Calculate the work done in pumping 10 000N of water from the lower reservoir through a distance of 100m to the upper reservoir.

   _____

   _____

HT
6 The power output of a crane is 1.6kW. Calculate how long it will take to lift a load of 5000N through a distance of 8m.

_____

1 **a)** What is kinetic energy? ....

b) A truck of mass 2000kg and a car of mass 1000kg are travelling down a motorway at the same speed.

i) Which one has the greatest kinetic energy? ....

ii) Explain your answer. ....

c) Two cars of the same mass are travelling down a road. Explain how one car could have more kinetic energy than the other.

....

....

2 For the following pairs of objects, state which has the most kinetic energy and give a brief reason why:

a) A car of mass 1000kg or a lorry of mass 3200kg, both moving at 10m/s.

....

b) Car A of mass 100kg moving at 15m/s or Car B of mass 1000kg moving at 10m/s.

....

3 Why is it not fair to say that electric cars reduce pollution?

....

....

HT

4 Calculate the kinetic energy of the following:

a) A car of mass 1000kg moving along a road at a constant speed of 20m/s.

....

....

b) A truck of mass 32 000kg moving along a road at a speed of 10m/s.

....

....

c) A skier of mass 90kg skiing down a hill at a speed of 15m/s.

....

....

d) A toy truck of mass 1300g moving at a speed of 30cm/s.

....

....

Crumple Zones

1 Seatbelts and air bags reduce the deceleration of the car in an accident. Is this statement **true** or **false**?

....

2 Explain why the following safety features are included in cars:

a) seatbelts ....

b) air bags ....

c) brakes ....

d) crumple zone ....

3 Why would the passenger section not be part of a car's crumple zones?

....

4 What is the difference between active and passive safety features in cars?

....

....

5 Explain the advantages of anti-lock braking systems over normal brakes.

....

....

6 Which passive safety feature do you think prevents the most accidents? Explain your choice.

....

....

HT

7 The stopping forces experienced by a passenger during a crash can be reduced by increasing the collision time. Choose a safety feature which performs this task and describe how it works.

....

....

1 When terminal speed is reached, which two forces are balanced?

....

2 A skydiver of weight 700N steps out of a plane.

a) What causes the skydiver to fall? ....

b) When the skydiver steps out of the plane she initially accelerates. Explain, in terms of the forces acting on the skydiver, why she accelerates.

....

c) What happens to the weight of the skydiver as she falls? ....

d) What will happen to the value of the air resistance as she falls? Why does this happen?

....

e) Eventually the skydiver will fall at a steady speed. Explain, in terms of the forces acting on the skydiver, why she falls at a steady speed.

....

....

f) Eventually, after she has reached a terminal speed, the skydiver opens her parachute. What effect will this have on the air resistance acting on her?

....

3 The table below shows the speed of a skydiver at 5-second intervals after she steps out of a plane, up to the point where she opens her parachute.

Time (s)	0	5	10	15	20	25	30	35	40	45	50
Speed (m/s)	0	10	19	27	33	36	38	39	40	40	40

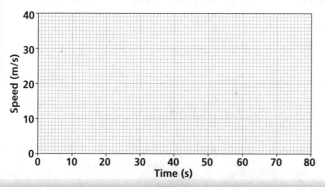

a) Draw a speed–time graph of the falling skydiver on the axes opposite.

b) The skydiver eventually comes to a rest on the ground after 78s. On the axes opposite complete the graph, showing how her speed might change after 50s (when she opens her parachute).

The Energy of Games and Theme Rides

1 a) What is gravitational potential energy?

....

b) Give two examples of objects that have gravitational potential energy.

....

2 The diagrams alongside show a ball on a slope. **A** 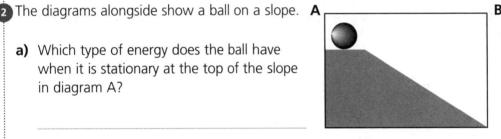 **B**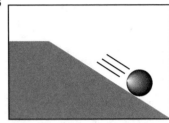

a) Which type of energy does the ball have when it is stationary at the top of the slope in diagram A?

....

b) Which types of energy does the ball have when it is rolling down the slope in diagram B?

....

HT

3 A cyclist climbs up a hill from a height of 100m to a height of 300m. The cyclist has a mass of 70kg. By how much does the cyclist's gravitational potential energy increase? (Remember: formula, working and unit.)

....

....

4 An electric motor of power rating 4000W lifts a load of 400N. It takes 10s to lift the load.

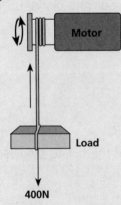

a) What is the main energy change that is taking place?

....

b) If the motor is 100% efficient, how much energy does the motor transfer to the load? (Remember: formula, working and unit.)

....

....

c) What height is the load lifted through? (Remember: formula, working and unit.)

....

The Energy of Games and Theme Rides

1 In the space below, sketch the shape of a roller-coaster in which the following energy changes take place:
- First, there is a gradual transfer of electrical energy to gravitational potential energy.
- This gravitational potential energy is then swiftly transferred into kinetic energy.
- The kinetic energy remains constant for a period of time before transferring back into gravitational potential energy again.

2 If a roller-coaster designer wishes to increase the maximum kinetic energy of the cars, which should he double: their mass or the speed? Explain your answer.

....

....

3 If you moved a roller-coaster ride to the moon, how would the ride be different and why?

....

....

HT

4 Explain how the kinetic and gravitational potential energy of an object may vary when it is falling at its terminal speed.

....

....

5 Two masses are shown below. Calculate their weight on Earth. (g = 10m/s^2 or 10N/kg)

a) Mass = 2kg ....   **b)** Mass = 10kg ....

....

Who Planted That There?

1 The diagram shows the structure of a leaf. Label it using the words from the following list:

Waxy cuticle
Guard cells
Stomata
Palisade cells
Spongy mesophyll layer
Epidermis

2 Write down four ways in which a leaf is adapted for photosynthesis. For each one, explain how the adaptation benefits the leaf.

3 A plant needs water and carbon dioxide for photosynthesis. It produces oxygen as a waste product.

a) State where each substance below enters or exits the plant.

i) Water

ii) Carbon dioxide

iii) Oxygen

b) What is the name of the process by which carbon dioxide and oxygen enter or exit the plant?

Water, Water Everywhere

1 a) What is meant by the term 'osmosis'?

_____

b) The diagram below shows an experiment that can be carried out to demonstrate osmosis. Explain the results in detail.

Thistle funnel

30 mins later

Sugar solution

Visking tubing

Pure water

_____

_____

_____

_____

c) Insert a tick (✓) or a cross (✗) to indicate whether the following are examples of osmosis.

i) Water evaporating from leaves. ☐

ii) Water moving from plant cell to plant cell. ☐

iii) Mixing pure water and sugar solution. ☐

iv) A pear losing water in a concentrated solution. ☐

v) Water moving from blood to body cells. ☐

vi) Sugar being absorbed from the intestine into the blood. ☐

2 Tick the statement below which best describes what happens during osmosis.

a) All water particles move from an area of high concentration to an area of low concentration. ☐

b) Most water particles move from an area of high concentration to an area of low concentration but some move the opposite way. ☐

c) All water particles move from an area of low concentration to an area of high concentration. ☐

3 Root hair cells absorb water from the soil. Use your understanding of osmosis to explain how this happens.

_____

_____

Water, Water Everywhere

1 Plants require a constant supply of water. List four ways in which a plant uses this water.

....

2 Blood cells also absorb and lose water by osmosis from their surroundings. Draw a diagram of red blood cells to help you explain what the blood cells would look like in the following samples:

    a) A normal blood sample where the red blood cells are bathed in plasma (which is the same concentration as their cytoplasm).

    b) A blood sample from an athlete who has just run a marathon and is dehydrated.

    c) A blood sample from a hospital patient who has accidentally been given a transfusion of pure water instead of saline.

a)	b)	c)

HT

3 Plant cells would not burst if surrounded by pure water. Why is this?

....

....

4 Why do plant cells behave in a different way to animal cells when they are in a high concentration of water?

....

5 Explain what the following terms mean:

    a) Plasmolysis: ....

    b) Lysis: ....

    c) Crenated: ....

Transport in Plants

1 Two of the main organs of a flowering plant are named in the table below.
Name each organ's main component(s) and state what function(s) it performs.

Organ	Main Component(s)	Function(s)
Stem	1. _____ 2. _____	1. _____ 2. Transports water and minerals from roots to leaves.
Leaves	1. _____	1. _____

2 a) Label the different tube systems in the vascular bundle in the diagram below.

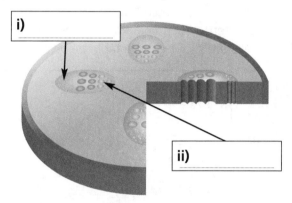

i) _____

ii) _____

b) State the function of each tube system.

i) Name: _____

Function: _____

ii) Name: _____

Function: _____

3 The diagram shows an experiment that can be carried out to investigate the water taken up by a plant.
The results table is shown below.

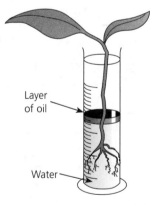

Layer of oil

Water

Time (in days)	0	1	2	3	4
Volume of water in cylinder (cm³)	50	47	43	42	40

a) Why was a layer of oil placed in the measuring cylinder?

_____

b) What happened to the volume of water in the measuring cylinder? _____

c) How would you expect the results to have changed if...

i) the plant had been in a colder room? _____

ii) the plant had been in a more humid atmosphere? _____

iii) air had been blown over the leaves of the plant? _____

Plants Need Minerals Too

1 Draw lines between the boxes to connect each essential mineral with its function and the symptoms that would be shown by the plant if that mineral was deficient.

Essential Minerals	Main Function	Symptoms Caused by Deficiency
Potassium	Photosynthesis and respiration	Stunted root growth and discoloured leaves
Magnesium	Respiration and cell growth	Undeveloped fruit and flowers and discoloured leaves
Phosphates	Making proteins	Stunted growth and yellow leaves
Nitrates	Photosynthesis	Yellow leaves

2 A group of students investigated the effect that the mass of fertiliser used would have on the yield of barley. They planted five fields of barley, added differing amounts of fertiliser to each field and five months later measured the amount of barley produced in each field. The results are shown in the table below.

Mass of Fertiliser Used (kg)	0	50	100	150	200
Yield of Barley (Tonnes)	18	27	34	38	38

a) Draw a line graph to show the results of the table on the graph paper provided.

b) State two variables the scientists needed to control to ensure it was a fair test.

c) Which of the above fields was used as a 'control'?

d) What yield of barley would have been produced by 75kg of fertiliser?

e) What yield of barley would have been produced by 250kg of fertiliser?

HT

3 a) What is meant by the term 'concentration gradient'?

b) What is meant by the term 'active transport'?

c) Explain why a root hair cell must absorb ions by active transport.

1 **a)** The following information describes 'what eats what' in a habitat. Use it to draw a food chain in the box below.

Dormice eat barley.
Dormice are eaten by stoats.
Foxes eat stoats.

b) Label the stages in the food chain above with the following terms:

producer **herbivore** **carnivore** **primary consumer** **top carnivore**

c) What is the original source of energy for the food chain?

2 **a)** What is the difference between a pyramid of numbers and a pyramid of biomass?

b) Draw a pyramid of numbers for the following food chain:

Rose Bush → Greenfly →
Ladybird → Tree Creeper (Bird)

c) Draw a pyramid of biomass for the same food chain.

Energy Flow

1 The diagram alongside shows the energy intake and usage for a cow.

a) Where does the cow's energy intake come from?

....

b) What are the two main types of energy that account for the 2000kJ transferred by the cow?

....

....

c) How much of the energy taken in by the cow is 'used' for new growth?

....

....

2000kJ transferred by the cow

6000kJ intake

New growth

3000kJ in faeces

2 a) What is 'biomass'?

....

....

b) Name three sources of biomass which can be used as fuels.

....

....

....

....

HT

3 Use the formula below to calculate the efficiency of energy transfer for the cow in the diagram above.

$$\text{Energy efficiency} = \frac{\text{Energy used usefully (for new growth)}}{\text{Energy taken in}} \times 100\%$$

....

4 a) Why is it more efficient for a human to be a vegetarian?

....

....

b) Why are most animals that are eaten by humans herbivores rather than carnivores?

....

....

Farming

1 a) What are pesticides? ....

b) Give three problems with using pesticides.

....

c) What are herbicides? ....

d) What are some of the problems associated with the use of herbicides?

....

e) Why has the use of pesticides and herbicides become more widespread?

....

f) Why do you think there is an increasing number of people who buy organically produced foodstuffs (i.e. foods that are produced without chemicals)?

....

2 A farmer breeds cows for beef. The animals are kept in enclosures inside a barn to regulate the temperature and to prevent the animals from moving around too much.

a) In terms of food production, explain why the farmer would want to...

i) regulate the temperature of the environment in which the cows are kept.

....

....

ii) restrict how much the cows can move around.

....

....

b) Suggest one other advantage of keeping the cows inside a barn like this.

....

c) Suggest one disadvantage of raising the cows in this way. ....

d) Some people object to livestock being raised in this way. Suggest one reason for this.

....

Farming

1 Organic farmers do not use chemical fertilisers. Describe two ways that they can fertilise their crops.

_____

_____

_____

2 Organic farmers do not use chemical pesticides or herbicides to kill pests or weeds.

a) How do they control weeds? _____

_____

b) How do they control insect pests? _____

_____

3 A farmer grows tomatoes in huge greenhouses. He uses a hydroponics system to grow the plants.

a) What is meant by 'hydroponics'? _____

b) Describe one advantage to the farmer of growing tomatoes in this way.

_____

c) The greenhouse environment enables the farmer to control the environmental conditions for fast, intensive growth. Name three conditions and explain how they might be controlled:

Condition	Method of Control

HT

4 Suggest two advantages and two disadvantages of growing a tomato crop using the hydroponics system.

Advantages: _____

Disadvantages: _____

Decay

1 List three optimum conditions that decomposers need in order to thrive and cause decay.

_____

2 Detritivores make the decay process even faster.

a) Give two examples of detritivores.

_____

b) Explain how detritivores increase the rate of decay.

_____

_____

3 Describe four methods of preserving food and explain how they work to prevent the growth of decomposer microorganisms.

_____

_____

_____

_____

HT

4 A Year 11 class were set a task of designing and making a composter. Two designs are shown below.

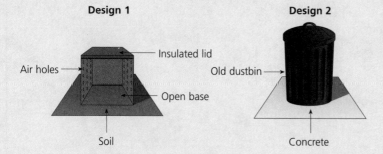

In which composter will the best compost be made? Give three reasons.

_____

_____

_____

5 Decomposers and detritivores are saprophytes. Describe how they feed on waste material.

_____

_____

Recycling

1 What does the term 'recycling' mean?

_____

2 Write the appropriate number alongside each explanation below, to show which stage of the carbon cycle it is describing.

a) Animals release CO_2 (a product of respiration) into the air. ☐

b) Microorganisms break down excrement and the bodies of dead animals and plants. ☐

c) Green plants take CO_2 from the atmosphere for photosynthesis. Some is returned during respiration. ☐

d) Microorganisms release CO_2 (a product of respiration) into the air. ☐

e) Carbon is converted into carbohydrates, fats and proteins by plants. When the plant is eaten, some of this carbon is then converted into carbohydrates, fats and proteins in the animal. ☐

HT

3 a) Construct your own carbon cycle for carbon-recycling in the sea, using the boxes below:

| CO_2 in air | CO_2 dissolved in sea water | Carbon in phytoplankton (microscopic plants) | Carbon in marine animals | Carbon in limestone rock |

b) Add the names of these processes to your diagram of the carbon cycle:

| Respiration | Photosynthesis | Death | Fossilisation |

1 The diagram below is a simplified version of the nitrogen cycle.

a) Describe what occurs in each of the stages in the nitrogen cycle.

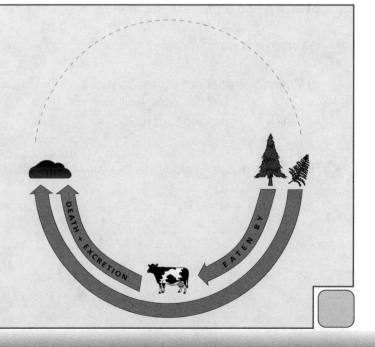

Stage 1: ....

....

Stage 2: ....

....

Stage 3: ....

....

Stage 4: ....

....

Stage 5: ....

....

b) Leguminous plants (e.g. beans and clover) contain nitrogen-fixing bacteria in small nodules attached to their roots. Why are leguminous plants sometimes grown by farmers only to be ploughed in?

....

....

HT

2 a) Complete the more advanced version of the nitrogen cycle alongside.

b) Show on your diagram where the following soil microorganisms are involved in the nitrogen cycle:

Decomposers (bacteria and fungi)
Nitrifying bacteria
Denitrifying bacteria
Nitrogen-fixing bacteria

Fundamental Chemical Concepts

HT

1 a) What is the formula for ammonia? ....

b) What is the formula for ammonium chloride? ....

c) What is the difference between the formula of ammonia and that of ammonium?

....

d) The formula of ammonium sulfate is $(NH_4)_2SO_4$. How many atoms of each element does it contain?

N ....

H ....

S ....

O ....

2 This is a word equation for a common neutralisation reaction. Write the formulae for it underneath.

Sodium hydroxide + Hydrochloric acid ⟶ Sodium chloride + Water

.... + ... ⟶ .... + ...

3 For each question below, select your answer from the following formulae.

CuO Na_2CO_3 $BaCl_2$ $BaSO_4$ $AgNO_3$ KOH $(NH_4)_2SO_4$ H_2SO_4

a) Which one contains silver? ....

b) Which one contains only 2 atoms? ....

c) Which one is a carbonate? ....

d) Which one does not contain oxygen? ....

e) Which one contains 6 atoms? ....

4 Fill in the formulae underneath this common neutralisation reaction.

Silver nitrate + Sodium chloride ⟶ Silver chloride + Sodium nitrate

.... + ... ⟶ .... + $NaNO_3$

1 a) What is an acid?

....

b) What is a base?

....

c) Complete the general equation:

Acid + Base ⟶ .... + ...

2 A beaker containing 100cm³ of sodium hydroxide had universal indicator solution added to it. Sulfuric acid was then added using a burette and the pH of the solution was estimated by gauging the colour of the liquid. The solution was constantly stirred. The results are shown below.

Volume of Acid Added (cm³)	0	4	12	30	50
pH of Solution	14	12	10	8	7

a) Plot a graph of the results.

b) What colour was the solution at the start?

....

c) What colour was the solution at the end? ....

d) What is the name given to this type of reaction?

....

e) Write a word equation for the reaction taking place.

....

f) Write a symbol equation for the reaction taking place.

....

3 Complete the general equation.

Acid + Carbonate ⟶ .... + ... + ...

Acids and Bases

HT

1 Draw lines between the boxes to link them correctly.

| Alkali | Hydrogen ions | $OH^-_{(aq)}$ |

| Acid | Hydroxide ions | $H^+_{(aq)}$ |

2 Complete the ionic equation that describes neutralisation.

.... + ... $\longrightarrow$ $H_2O_{(l)}$

3 For each reaction below...
i) complete the word equation
ii) write a balanced symbol equation, including state symbols.

a) i) Sodium hydroxide + Hydrochloric acid $\longrightarrow$ .... + Water

ii) .... + ... $\longrightarrow$ .... + ...

b) i) Copper (II) oxide + Sulfuric acid $\longrightarrow$ .... + ...

ii) .... + ... $\longrightarrow$ .... + ...

c) i) Ammonia + Nitric acid $\longrightarrow$ ....

ii) .... + ... $\longrightarrow$ ....

d) i) Calcium carbonate + ... $\longrightarrow$ Calcium chloride + ... + ...

ii) .... + ... $\longrightarrow$ .... + ... + ...

e) i) .... + ... $\longrightarrow$ Copper (II) nitrate + Water

ii) .... + ... $\longrightarrow$ .... + ...

f) i) Calcium carbonate + ... $\longrightarrow$ Calcium nitrate + ...

ii) .... + ... $\longrightarrow$ .... + ...

g) i) Potassium hydroxide + Sulfuric acid $\longrightarrow$ .... + ...

ii) .... + ... $\longrightarrow$ .... + ...

h) i) .... + Hydrochloric acid $\longrightarrow$ Sodium chloride + ... + ...

ii) .... + ... $\longrightarrow$ .... + ... + ...

Reacting Masses

1 Use the periodic table (on p.96) to find the relative atomic mass of the following elements:

a) Beryllium ....
b) Aluminium ....
c) Chlorine ....
d) Bromine ....

2 Use the periodic table to help you calculate the relative formula mass of the following compounds:

a) Copper oxide, CuO

b) Sodium chloride, NaCl

c) Water, H_2O

d) Ethene, C_2H_4

e) Calcium hydroxide, $Ca(OH)_2$

f) Sulfuric acid, H_2SO_4

3 For each of the following compounds, 'X' is an unknown element. The relative formula mass of the compound is given in the bracket. Work out which element X represents.

a) XO (40) ....

b) XCl_2 (111) ....

c) CX_2 (44) ....

d) XNO_3 (63) ....

e) XO_2 (62) ....

4 Potassium nitrate fertiliser is made by reacting nitric acid with potassium hydroxide.

Potassium hydroxide + Nitric acid ⟶ Potassium nitrate + Water

They react in the following ratio 56 : 63 : 101 : 18

a) 28g of potassium hydroxide is reacted with 31.5g of nitric acid. How much potassium nitrate would be made?

....

b) How much nitric acid you would need to start with in order to make 505 tonnes of potassium nitrate?

....

....

Reacting Masses

1 Calcium carbonate and hydrochloric acid react together to produce calcium chloride, carbon dioxide and water.

a) Work out the M_r for each of the reactants and products in the equation and write them underneath.

$$CaCO_{3(s)} + 2HCl_{(aq)} \longrightarrow CaCl_{2(aq)} + CO_{2(g)} + H_2O_{(l)}$$

_____

b) What is the total mass of the reactants? _____

c) What is the total mass of the products? _____

d) Would you have expected the masses in part b) and part c) to be the same?

_____

e) What mass of calcium chloride can be produced from 2g of calcium carbonate?

_____

_____

f) A tonne of calcium carbonate is fully reacted with hydrochloric acid. What mass of water is produced?

_____

_____

g) What mass of hydrochloric acid would be needed to fully react with 25g of calcium carbonate?

_____

_____

2 Ammonia and sulfuric acid react together to make ammonium sulfate.

a) Work out the M_r for each of the reactants and products in the equation and write them underneath.

$$2NH_{3(aq)} + H_2SO_{4(aq)} \longrightarrow (NH_4)_2SO_{4(aq)}$$

_____

b) What mass of ammonium sulfate can be produced from 68g of ammonia?

_____

Reacting Masses

1 Which of the three statements below correctly defines the term 'percentage yield'?

a) The amount of product that you use. ☐

b) The amount of product obtained from a reaction. ☐

c) The amount of reactant left over from a reaction. ☐

2 Complete the following table. The first one has been done for you.

Actual Yield	Predicted Yield	Percentage Yield
12g	20g	$\frac{12g \times 100\%}{20g} = 60\%$
6g	8g	
1.2g	1.8g	
44kg	44kg	
0.8g	6.4g	
	25kg	50%
63g		90%

3 An experiment was carried out to produce copper sulfate (a salt). The method used is outlined below. The actual yield of copper sulfate was 4.2g; the predicted yield was 5g.

Copper Oxide

Add excess copper oxide, then filter to remove any unreacted copper oxide.

Sulfuric Acid

Evaporate to leave behind blue crystals of the 'salt' copper sulfate.

a) State the equation used to calculate percentage yield. ....

b) Calculate the percentage yield of copper sulfate. ....

c) Give three reasons why the percentage yield of copper sulfate is less than 100%.

....

d) What would you expect the percentage yield to be if excess copper oxide was added to twice the volume of sulfuric acid? Explain your answer.

....

Fertilisers and Crop Yield

1 This is a label on a bag of fertiliser.

> **Contents**
> N (20%), P (10%), K (10%)

a) What do the letters N, P and K stand for?

....

b) Why are these elements put in fertilisers?

....

....

c) Why do farmers use fertilisers?

....

....

2 Use letters to indicate which reactants from the list below you would use in order to make the following fertilisers (you can use a letter more than once):

A Nitric acid
B Potassium hydroxide
C Sulfuric acid
D Ammonia
E Phosphoric acid

a) Ammonium sulfate ☐ ☐

b) Potassium nitrate ☐ ☐

c) Ammonium phosphate ☐ ☐

3 Calculate the relative formula mass of the following fertilisers:

a) Ammonium chloride, NH_4Cl

....

....

b) Potassium nitrate, KNO_3

....

....

Fertilisers and Crop Yield

1 Why is it important for fertilisers to provide nitrogen in the form of soluble nitrates?

_____

2 The diagram shows an arable (crop-growing) farm. The farm is intensively farmed and the farmer uses a lot of fertiliser to increase his yields.

Water from the farm drains into the stream labelled A. This then drains into the River at B (which flows from left to right). The river has an abundance of fish at X. However, anglers are increasingly complaining about the lack of fish at Z.

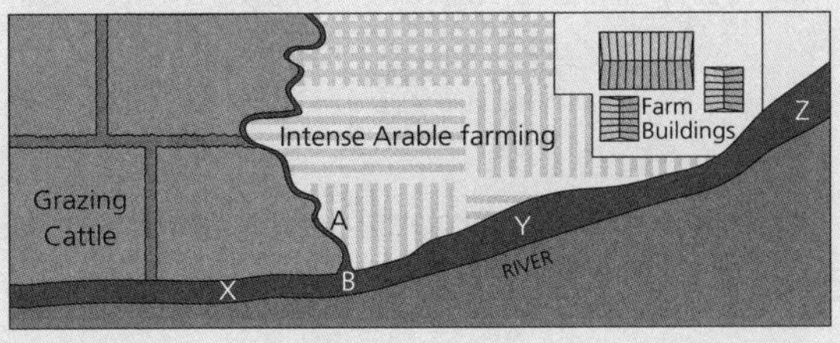

a) Explain why you would find a lot of growth of simple algae at Y.

_____

b) Explain how this growth of simple algae can eventually affect the population of fish in the river at Z.

_____

_____

_____

_____

c) What is the name given to the process described above?_____

3 a) What is the formula used to calculate the percentage mass of an element in a compound?

Percentage mass = _____

b) Calculate the percentage mass of nitrogen in the following fertilisers:

   i) Ammonium chloride, NH_4Cl

_____

_____

   ii) Ammonium nitrate, NH_4NO_3

_____

_____

   iii) Ammonium sulfate, $(NH_4)_2SO_4$

_____

   iv) Ammonium phosphate, $(NH_4)_3PO_4$

_____

Making Ammonia – Haber Process & Costs

1 The following questions all relate to the Haber process.

a) Where is the nitrogen (a raw material) obtained from?

....

b) Why are the nitrogen and hydrogen passed over iron?

....

c) How is the ammonia separated from the other gases at the end of the process?

....

....

d) The production of ammonia is an example of a reversible reaction. Explain what this means.

....

e) Why are the optimum conditions not used in the Haber process?

....

2 The graph below shows the percentage yield of a reaction at different temperatures and pressures.

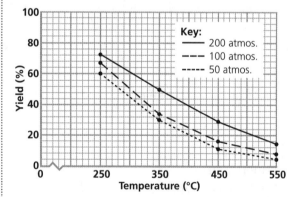

a) What temperature gives the highest yield?................................

b) What is the yield at a pressure of 200 atmospheres and a temperature of 350°C?

....

c) What happens to the yield as the temperature is increased?

....

3 Outline three costs that are involved in making ammonia in the Haber process.

....

....

....

....

Making Ammonia – Haber Process & Costs

1 a) The standard pressure for the Haber process is 200 atmospheres. Outline two costs in maintaining such a high pressure.

....

....

b) Catalysts are expensive. How do they reduce costs in the long run?

....

c) What is the benefit of automating the Haber process?

....

HT

2 The main reaction in the manufacture of sulfuric acid (the contact process) is the oxidation of sulfur dioxide to make sulfur trioxide.

$$2SO_{2(g)} + O_{2(g)} \rightleftharpoons 2SO_{3(g)}$$

The reaction uses a catalyst, vanadium oxide (VO), and is carried out at 4500°C, at just above atmospheric pressure. The yield under these conditions is 98%. (Remember you do not have to remember any of these details, you just need to use them to answer the following questions.)

a) How does using a catalyst affect the rate of the reaction?

....

b) How does using a catalyst affect the yield of the reaction?

....

c) How would increasing the temperature of the reaction affect the yield?

....

d) What would be the disadvantage of reducing the temperature?

....

e) i) Increasing the pressure would increase the yield. Explain why this is true for this reaction.

....

ii) Why is the reaction carried out at a fairly low pressure?

....

Detergents

1 What is the purpose of adding the following ingredients to a detergent in a washing powder?

a) Bleach: ....

b) Optical brightener: ....

c) Enzyme: ....

2 Look at the following washing symbols below and write down the conditions that should be used to wash a garment.

a)

b)

c)

....

3 What is the purpose of adding the following ingredients to a detergent in a washing-up liquid?

a) Rinse agent: ....

b) Water softener: ....

c) Fragrance: ....

4 A student made up four solutions of a biological washing powder. She used 50ml of water each time but changed the amount of washing powder she used to make different concentrations. In each one, she put a small piece of photographic film, which had a coating made of a protein that is broken down by the enzymes in the washing powder. She timed how long it took the washing powder to break up the coating.

Amount of Biological Washing Powder Used (g)	1	2	3	4	5
Time Taken to Break Down Protein (s)	340	125	62	62	62

a) Plot the results on the graph paper provided.

b) How does the ability of the solution to remove the protein change as more powder was added?

....

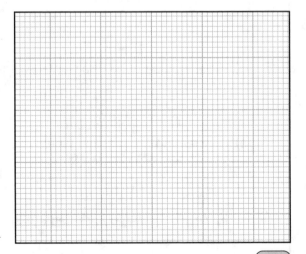

Detergents

1. Explain the meaning of the following words

   a) Hydrophobic: ....

   b) Hydrophilic: ....

2. Label the hydrophilic and hydrophobic parts of the detergent molecule below.

   ┌────────────────────────────────┐   ┌────────────────────────────────┐
   │ .... │   │ .... │
   └────────────────────────────────┘   └────────────────────────────────┘

3. Use the diagrams below to explain how washing-up liquid will remove grease from a plate.

   ....

   ....

   ....

4. Marilyn found that the grease stain on her dress would not come off using water. She used a dry-cleaning solvent and it came off easily. Use your understanding of intermolecular forces to explain why.

   ....

   ....

   ....

Batch or Continuous

1 Link the following statements to either a batch process or a continuous process as appropriate.

| Reactor never stops. |
| Labour intensive. |
| Can work on a small scale. |
| Can be used to make different substances. |
| Runs automatically. |
| Only makes one product. |

Batch

Continuous

2 Decide whether each of the following is a continuous or a batch process:

a) Making a cake ....

b) Fractional distillation of crude oil ....

c) Making ammonium sulfate in a school laboratory ....

d) The Haber process ....

3 Chlorophyll is soluble in ethanol. Describe a method you would use to extract chlorophyll from the leaves of a plant.

....

....

4 The development of a medicine might go through the following stages:
a) Discovery of a plant material with some medicinal effect.
b) Collection of plant and extraction of material.
c) Changing material chemically to improve it.
d) Making medicine synthetically by the cheapest method.

Outline a cost involved in each stage and indicate why it would be expensive.

....

....

....

1 Connect the statements to the substance to which it applies. (Some sentences may apply to more than one substance.)

Very high melting point.

Soft.

Does not conduct electricity.

| Diamond |

Contains carbon atoms bonded to each other.

| Graphite |

Very hard.

Conducts electricity.

2 a) Label the structures alongside using the following words (you will need to use some labels more than once):
Strong covalent bond
Weak intermolecular bond
Carbon
Graphite
Diamond

i)

ii)

b) Describe the structure of each substance in part a) above.

i) _____

ii) _____

c) With reference to the structure of the molecules, explain why...

i) diamond has a very high melting point.

_____

ii) graphite conducts electricity but diamond does not.

_____

3 What is an allotrope?

_____

_____

Nanochemistry

1 Complete the sentences using two of the words below:

small   **allotrope**   **atomic**   **viscous**

Nanochemistry deals with chemistry on an .... scale. This means sizes of around 1

nanometre (0.000000001m). This is very, very ....

2 a) What is the name of this form of carbon shown opposite?

....

b) What is its formula? ....

c) What colour is it...

i) when it is solid? ....

ii) when it is dissolved in petrol? ....

3 a) What is a nanotube?

....

b) Nanotubes have two important physical properties, what are they?

....

4 The uses of nanotubes are still being researched. Give two uses that have been developed.

....

....

....

....

5 Using nanotubes and fullerenes to cage materials is an exciting development. Outline one area where this is being researched.

....

....

....

How Pure is Our Water?

1 a) Unscramble the words to reveal four sources of water.

i) SIRREV ....   **ii)** IFISQUARE ....

iii) SKALE ....   **iv)** RIVERROSES ....

b) Give three uses for water.

....

....

....

2 The pie chart alongside shows the sources of water in Northern Ireland.

a) What is the main source of water in Northern Ireland?

....

b) What is the total percentage of the supply that comes from lakes, loughs and reservoirs?

....

Key: ■ Reservoirs 47%
■ Groundwater 6%
■ Rivers 6%
■ Lakes/Loughs 41%

c) If you drew a pie chart for the water supply for Southern England, would you expect it to be different? Explain your answer.

....

....

3 Why is access to clean water so important, especially to people in the developing world?

....

....

4 Raw water is treated before it reaches our homes. What is the name of the process that is used at the water works to…

a) remove fine suspended particles? ....

b) kill any harmful bacteria? ....

c) allow insoluble particles to settle? ....

How Pure is Our Water?

1 Outline two sources of pollution in drinking water and suggest for each one how it might be reduced.

_____

_____

_____

_____

_____

2 a) What is a precipitate? _____

b) What happens in a precipitation reaction? _____

3 David dissolves a potassium salt in water. When he adds a small sample of barium chloride solution to the solution of the potassium salt, a white precipitate is formed.

a) What is the chemical name of the white precipitate? _____

b) What is the full name of the potassium salt? _____

c) Write a word equation for the reaction including state symbols.

_____

HT

d) Write a symbol equation for the reaction including state symbols.

_____

4 a) Emily needs a sample of pure water. What is the name of the method she would use to prepare a sample of pure water from tap water?

_____

b) Why is tap water not made by this method?

_____

c) Georgie thinks that the world shortage of clean drinking water can be solved by treating sea water as 70% of the world is covered by sea water. Explain to her why this is not possible on a large scale.

_____

_____

1 Describe a situation where the build up of static electricity may lead to an explosion.

....

....

....

2 List three situations where static electricity is a nuisance but not a danger.

....

....

....

....

3 Hugh did an experiment in which he charged up two polythene rods and one Perspex rod by rubbing them with a cloth. The charge on the rods is shown in the diagram below.

Polythene rod rubbed with a cloth   Perspex rod rubbed with a cloth

a) He suspended the charged Perspex rod and one of the charged polythene rods. He then moved the other charged polythene rod towards the suspended rods.
Complete the sentences below to describe what would happen:

i) When he brought the charged polythene rod close to the charged Perspex rod…

....

ii) When he brought the charged polythene rod close to the charged polythene rod…

....

b) What can we conclude from this?

....

HT

c) Explain how the rods became charged.

....

Uses of Electrostatics

1 The following statements describe how a photocopier works.

A   Charged impression of the plate attracts tiny specs of black powder.
B   Paper is heated to fix the final image.
C   Copying plate is electrically charged.
D   Powder is transferred from the plate to the paper.
E   Image of the page to be copied is projected onto the plate.
F   Charge leaks away due to light, leaving an electrostatic impression of page.

Rearrange the statements to describe how a photocopier works.

☐   ☐   ☐   ☐   ☐   ☐

2 Describe, in detail, how a laser printer works.

_____

_____

_____

_____

3 How can static electricity be used to help someone whose heart has stopped?

_____

_____

_____

4 Fitting dust precipitators to a chimney causes most of the dust to collect at the bottom of the chimney rather than escaping into the atmosphere. Describe how this works.

_____

_____

_____

5 Bicycles can be painted using an electrostatic paint spray. The paint is given a positive charge.

a) What charge should the bike be given? Explain your answer. _____

_____

b) What is the advantage of using this method? _____

_____

Safe Electricals

1 The diagram shows a circuit breaker.

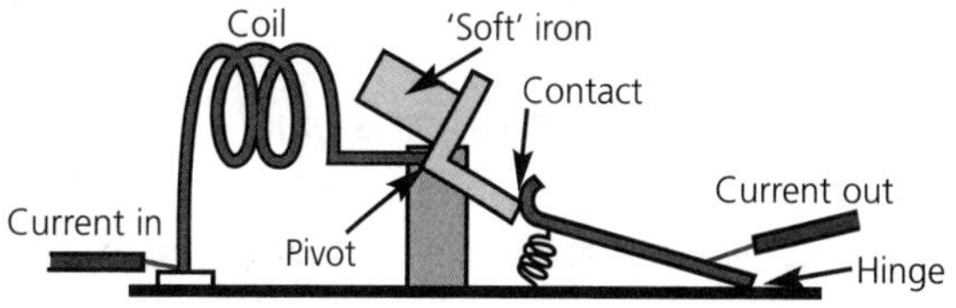

a) What is the job of a circuit breaker?

....

....

Labels on diagram: Coil | 'Soft' iron | Contact | Current in | Pivot | Current out | Hinge

b) What is the advantage of having a circuit breaker rather than a fuse?

....

....

2 Describe what might happen if a fault occurs in an electrical appliance that is being used without a fuse or a circuit breaker.

....

....

....

3 How does a fuse work?

....

....

....

....

HT

4 a) The diagram shows a hairdryer that has a plastic casing. The hairdryer plug only has two wires. Which two wires does it have?

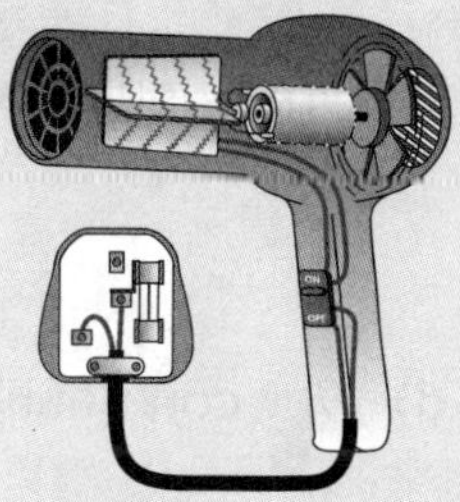

....

b) Which of the usual three wires is missing?...

c) The hairdryer is safe to use without the third wire. Explain why.

....

....

Safe Electricals

1 Indicate whether the following statements are **true** or **false**.

a) The colour of the earth wire is blue. ....

b) The neutral wire carries current away from an appliance. ....

c) Appliances with outer metal cases have no earth wire. ....

d) The live wire carries current to the appliance. ....

e) All appliances have cables with three wires in them. ....

f) A fuse is always part of the live wire. ....

2 What does the term 'double insulated' mean? ....

....

HT

3 The diagram alongside shows a toaster with a stainless-steel casing.
The earth wire is connected to the outer casing of the toaster.

a) What is the purpose of the earth wire? ....

....

b) If the brown live wire became loose and touched the outer casing of the toaster, explain how the earth wire would make the appliance safe.

....

....

c) What would have happened if the earth wire was not connected to the outer casing of the toaster?

....

d) Why don't double insulated appliances need to be earthed? ....

....

e) Why are double insulated appliances still protected by a fuse?

....

1 What is resistance?

_____

_____

2 The circuit below is used to measure the resistance of a fixed resistor.

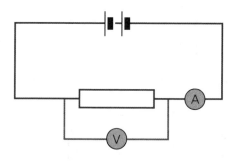

a) The reading on the voltmeter is 6V and the reading on the ammeter is 1.5A. Calculate the resistance of the resistor.

_____

_____

b) What would happen to the readings on the voltmeter and ammeter if one of the cells was removed? Explain your answer.

_____

_____

c) A different resistor was placed in the circuit. When the potential difference is 6V, the current flowing is 0.2A. Calculate the resistance of the resistor.

_____

HT

3 For the circuits shown below, each cell provides a potential difference of 1.5V. The total resistance of two resistors in series is simply their resistance added together. Complete the table below:

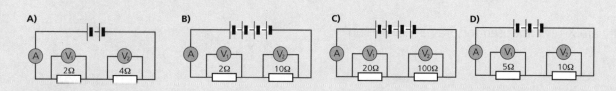

A)   B)   C)   D)

	Circuit A	Circuit B	Circuit C	Circuit D
p.d. supplied				
Total resistance				
Ammeter reading				
V_1				
V_2				

Ultrasound

1 One of the statements below is not true. Put a tick in the box to indicate which one.

   a) Ultrasound is high-frequency sound waves. ☐

   b) Ultrasound travels at the speed of light. ☐

   c) Ultrasound has a frequency greater than 20 000Hz. ☐

   d) Humans cannot hear ultrasound. ☐

2 Use the terms below to label the diagram.

Amplitude

Wavelength

3 Ultrasound scanning has reduced the need for some operations in hospitals. Why is this so?

....

....

4 How can ultrasound be used to remove kidney stones without opening up the patient?

....

....

5 Why are X-rays not used for pre-natal scanning?

....

HT

6 Using no more than four bullet points, explain how ultrasonic waves are used to build up a picture of the inside of the body.

....

....

....

Ultrasound

HT

1 Give two advantages of ultrasound over X-ray imaging.

....

....

2 How are ultrasound waves used to create an image?

....

....

....

3 a) Complete each diagram to show the way a slinky spring would behave if it is vibrated by someone's hand in the direction shown.

i)

ii)

b) On the longitudinal wave you have drawn, label where rarefaction and compression occur.

c) What type of wave is **a) ii)**?

....

d) Describe the movement of the particles in this wave.

....

....

e) Which of the waves generated in the above models could represent a light wave?

....

f) Draw on diagram **a) ii)** the movement of one particle in the wave.

Treatment

1 List three similarities between X-rays and gamma rays.

....

....

....

2 Rearrange the following word to reveal the name of the person in a hospital who takes X-rays.

PRODIHERRAGA ....

3 Describe two ways in which gamma rays can be used in hospitals.

....

....

....

HT

4 When electrons lose energy very quickly they emit electromagnetic radiation. Why are very high-speed electrons required to produce X-rays?

....

....

5 Explain why a nucleus may emit gamma radiation.

....

....

6 a) Gamma rays can be used to kill cancer cells. Explain, in as much detail as possible, how this process is carried out.

....

....

....

b) Gamma rays can also be a danger to health. Explain why.

....

....

What is Radioactivity?

1 Name the three types of radiation.

....

....

....

2 Put a tick in the box(es) next to the correct statement(s) below.

a) Radioactivity comes from the nucleus of an unstable atom. ☐

b) Radioactivity decreases with time. ☐

c) Radioactivity is measured by the total number of decays a material emits. ☐

HT

3 Complete the following sentences using the words below:

element   **neutrons**   **atomic**   **protons**   **mass**

After alpha emission, the new atom will have 2 fewer .... and 2 fewer ....

The .... number will have decreased by 2 and the .... number by 4.

The new atom is a different ....

4 After beta emission, the mass number of the atom remains the same, even though it becomes a new element. How is this so?

....

....

....

5 a) Radon-220 will decay into polonium-216. What kind of emission is this? Explain why.

....

....

b) Radon has an atomic number of 86. Use the information given in part **a)** to calculate the atomic number of polonium.

....

....

What is Radioactivity?

1 A radioisotope emits beta particles only. It has a half-life of 2 days.

Originally there is 200g of the active isotope. What mass of the isotope will remain radioactive after...

a) 2 days? ....

b) 4 days? ....

c) 8 days? ....

d) 16 days? ....

2 The table below shows the activity of a radioactive substance against time:

Time (mins)	0	2	4	6	8
Activity (Bq)	48	24	12	6	3

a) Draw a graph of activity against time.

b) What is the half-life of this radioactive substance?

....

3 Americium-241 is used in smoke detectors. It has a half-life of 460 years.

a) Why is it important for americium-241 to have a long half-life?

....

b) How long would it take americium-241 to decrease to one eighth of its original number of radioactive atoms?

....

4 Uranium isotopes decay to produce stable isotopes of lead. A sample of igneous rock is found to contain seven times as much lead as uranium. The half-life of uranium is 700 000 000 years. Calculate the age of the rock.

....

....

....

....

Uses of Radioisotopes

1 a) What is meant by the term 'background radiation'?

_____

b) Give three examples of background radiation. _____

2 Put a tick in the box next to the job below which is not carried out by tracers in industry.

Tracking the dispersal of waste. ☐   Finding leaks in underground pipes. ☐

Finding the routes taken by underground pipes. ☐   Finding cracks in metal structures. ☐

3 The diagram alongside shows a simple smoke detector.

a) Explain what happens when alpha particles pass between the two electrodes.

_____

_____

_____

α emitter
α particles
Alarm
Positive electrode
Negative electrode

b) Explain what subsequently happens if smoke enters the space between the two electrodes.

_____

_____

_____

4 Suggest why background radiation levels have increased in the last hundred years.

_____

_____

5 In no more than four bullet points, explain how tracers work in industry.

_____

_____

_____

_____

Fission

1 Explain how conventional power stations use fossil fuels to generate electricity.

_____

_____

2 The way nuclear power stations generate electricity is very similar to the way in which conventional power stations generate electricity. List three similarities.

_____

_____

_____

3 Explain what happens in a chain reaction.

_____

_____

HT

4 a) Nuclear fission can be used on a large scale in a nuclear reactor. Once fission has started it continues by itself. Explain why.

_____

_____

b) In a nuclear reactor, the reaction is controlled by control rods which 'absorb' neutrons. How would the 'absorption' of neutrons control the reaction?

_____

_____

c) What would happen if the reaction was not controlled by control rods?

_____

d) The energy released in each fission reaction is very small. How is it possible for a nuclear reactor to generate enormous amounts of energy?

_____

Across

3. The movement of a substance against a concentration gradient (6,9)

6. The number of waves produced in one second (9)

9. Cell division that forms daughter cells with half the number of chromosomes as the parent cell (7)

10. The type of electricity that is produced by friction and does not move from the object (6)

12. Name of a reaction between an acid and a base that forms a neutral solution (14)

13. The process by which an electric current causes a solution to undergo chemical decomposition (12)

14. A plant hormone that affects the growth and development of the plant (5)

Down

1. The maximum disturbance caused by a wave (9)

2. The distance between corresponding points on two adjacent disturbances (10)

4. The bond formed between two atoms in which both atoms share one or more pairs of electrons (8)

5. The movement of water through a partially permeable membrane from a high to a low concentration (7)

7. A measure of the state of motion of a body as a product of its mass and speed (8)

8. Cell division that forms two daughter cells, each with the same number of chromosomes as the parent cell (7)

11. A negatively charged particle found outside the nucleus of an atom (8)

Notes

Notes

Notes